Acknowledgements

The compilers and the publishers wish to thank the following for permission to use copyright material:

Ned Chalker, for *Everyday Things* by Jean Ayer.

David Higham Associates Ltd., for *Clothes* and *The Radio Men*, from 'The Secret Brother' by Elizabeth Jennings, published by Macmillan, London and Basingstoke. Also for *The Sounds in the Evening* by Eleanor Farjeon, from 'Silver Sand and Snow', published by Michael Joseph. Also for *Puffing Billy* by Christopher Hassall.

Stanley Cook, for *Soap, The Vacuum Cleaner, The Bus* and *The Road*, from 'Word Houses', and for *Letters, Going to the Launderette, How to Build a House* and *Television Aerials*, from 'Come Along'. Both books published by the author, 600 Barnsley Road, Sheffield, S5 6UA.

Dr. Jan Van Loewen Ltd., for *The Broken Toys* by James Kirkup.

Hodder and Stoughton Children's Books, for *Johnny's Pockets* by Alison Winn, from 'Helter Skelter and Tea With Me'.

Penguin Books Ltd., for *Flashlight*, from 'Flashlight and Other Poems' by Judith Thurman, published by Kestrel Books, 1977. © 1976 by Judith Thurman. Also for *Salford Road* and an extract from *Empty House*, from 'Salford Road' by Gareth Owen, published by Kestrel Books, 1979. Also for *There's a Red Brick Wall* by Nancy Chambers, from 'Stickleback, Stickleback', published by Kestrel Books, 1977. © Nancy Chambers 1977. Also for *Where?*, from 'Late Home' by Brian Lee, published by Kestrel Books, 1976. Copyright © Brian Lee.

William Jay Smith, for *The Toaster*, from 'Laughing Time: Nonsense Poems', published by Delacorte Press, 1980. © 1955, 1957, 1980 by William Jay Smith.

Jean Kenward, for *Breakdown*.

Faber and Faber Ltd., for *What Does the Clock Say?*, from 'Runes and Rhymes and Tunes and Chimes' by George Barker. Also for *Preludes 1*, from 'Collected Poems 1909–1962' by T.S. Eliot. Also for *The Night Mail*, from 'Collected Poems' by W.H. Auden. Also for *Surprise! Or the Escapologist*, from 'Bananas in Pyjamas' by Carey Blyton.

Michael Gibson, for *The Guillotine* by Wilfrid Gibson.

The National Trust and Macmillan, London Ltd., for an extract from *The Secret of the Machines* and for *The Way Through the Woods* by Rudyard Kipling, from 'The Definitive Edition of Rudyard Kipling's Verse'.

Blackie and Son Ltd., for an extract from *All Along the Street* by F.J. Teskey.

Margaret Greaves, for *City Lights*, from 'Your Turn Next', published by Methuen Educational Ltd., 1973. © Margaret Greaves 1966.

Marian Collihole, for *Church, School, Park and Shop*, from 'Themework', published by Stainer and Bell Ltd.

Marian Lines, for *Carbreakers, Building Site, Demolition of a Crescent* and *Looking Down on Roofs*, all from 'Tower Blocks' by Marian Lines, published by Franklin Watts Ltd.

Hubert Nicholson, Literary Executor, The Estate of A.S.J. Tessimond, and Autolycus Publications for *Summer Night at Hyde Park Corner* by A.S.J. Tessimond.

World's Work Ltd., for *The Old Coach Road, Pushcart Row* and *I'd Like to be a Lighthouse* by Rachel Field, from 'Poems for Children'. Poems selected from 'Taxis and Toadstools' by Rachel Field. Copyright 1926 by Doubleday and Co. Inc. Copyright 1924 by Yale Publishing Co. Copyright 1926 by Crowell Publishing Co. First published in Great Britain 1962 by World's Work Ltd. Also for *Houses*, from 'Taxis and Toadstools'. by Rachel Field. Copyright 1926 by Doubleday and Co. Inc. Copyright 1924 by Yale Publishing Co. Copyright 1926 by Crowell Publishing Co. Also for *Building a Skyscraper* by James S. Tippett, from 'Crickety Cricket! The Best-Loved Poems of James S. Tippett'. Text copyright © 1973 by Martha K. Tippett. First published in Great Britain 1975 by World's Work Ltd.

Holt, Rinehart and Winston, Publishers, for *Steam Shovel*, from 'Upper Pasture' by Charles Malam. Copyright 1930, © 1958 by Charles Malam.

Leslie Norris, for *The World of Hoardings* and *The Traffic Light*, both from 'Stories and Rhymes', BBC Radio, Spring 1972.

Oxford University Press, for *The Statue*, from 'The Blackbird in the Lilac' by James Reeves (1952).

Angus and Robertson (UK) Ltd., for *Pylons*, from 'And I Dance' by Keith Bosley.

Douglas Gibson, for *Piers*.

Miss Penelope Rieu, for *Portrait of a House* by E.V. Rieu.

Brian Lee, for *Sad ... and Glad*.

E.J. Arnold and Son Ltd., for *Empty House* by S. Gilman, from 'Poetry Corner'.

Harcourt Brace Jovanovich, Inc., for *The Concrete Highways* by Carl Sandburg, from 'Good Morning, America', copyright 1928, 1956 by Carl Sandburg.

Evans Brothers Ltd., for *The Song of the Engine* by H. Worsley-Benison, from 'The Book of a Thousand Poems'.

Bolt and Watson Ltd., for *Locomotive* by Shigeharu Nakano, from 'The Poetry of Living Japan'. Translated from the Japanese by Takamichi Ninomiya and D.J. Enright.

Dobson Books Ltd., for *Paper Boat and House*, from 'Collected Poems and Verses for Children' by Leonard Clark.

Samuel Menashe, for *A Flock of Little Boats*, from 'The Many Named Beloved' by Samuel Menashe.

Macmillan, London and Basingstoke, for *The Ship* by Sir John Squire, from 'Poetry Pack 1' edited by J. Gibson and R. Wilson.

Laurence Pollinger Ltd. and The Estate of Richard Church, for *The Ship* by Richard Church.

The Society of Authors as literary representative of the Estate of John Masefield, for *Sea-fever* and *Cargoes* by John Masefield.

Spike Milligan, for *A Baby Sardine*.

Gregory Harrison, for *Legging the Tunnel*, from 'A Second Book of Poetry', published by Oxford University Press. © Gregory Harrison. Also for *Helicopter*, from 'The Night of the Wild Horses', published by Oxford University Press. © Gregory Harrison.

Acknowledgements

Paul R. Reynolds, Inc., 12 East 41st Street, New York, N.Y. 10017, for *Flying* by Kaye Starbird. Copyright © 1963 by Kaye Starbird.

Derek Stuart, for *The Aeroplane,* from 'A First Poetry Book', published by Oxford University Press, and compiled by John L. Foster.

Ian Serraillier, for *The Helicopter.* © 1963 Ian Serraillier.

Edward Arnold (Publishers) Ltd., for *Uncle* by Harry Graham, from 'Most Ruthless Rhymes for Heartless Homes'.

Routledge and Kegan Paul Ltd., London, for *Space Travel* by Sylvia Leach, from 'Poems by Children', edited by Michael Baldwin (1962).

Modern Curriculum Press, for *Motor Cars,* from 'Songs from Around a Toadstool Table' by Rowena Bastin Bennett. Copyright © 1967 by Rowena Bastin Bennett. Also for *The Freight Train,* from 'The Day is Dancing and Other Poems' by Rowena Bastin Bennett. Copyright © 1968 by Rowena Bastin Bennett.

Frances Gorman Risser, for *City Beasts.*

We have been unable to trace the copyright owners of the following poems and should be pleased to hear from them or their heirs and assigns. In the meantime, we venture to include:

The Garden Hose by Beatrice Janosco
Wasteland by Mark Chaplin
London Eclogue by F. J. Osborn
The Rush Hour by Gillian Anderson
The Park by Olive Dehn
Change by Nick Godwin
The Excavator by N. Manton
The Cement Mixer by Hugh Eva
An extract from *Journey* by Harold Monro
The Aeroplane by Michael Jenkins

4

Contents

Contents

Contents

Everyday Things

Millionaires, presidents — even kings
Can't get along without everyday things.

Were you president, king or millionaire,
You'd use a comb to comb your hair.

If you wished to be clean — and you would, I hope
You'd take a bath with water and soap.

And you'd have to eat — if you wanted to eat —
Bread and vegetables, fish and meat;

While your drink for breakfast would probably be
Milk or chocolate, coffee or tea

You'd have to wear — you could hardly refuse —
Under clothes, outer clothes, stockings and shoes.

If you wished to make a reminding note,
You'd take a pencil out of your coat;

Everyday Things

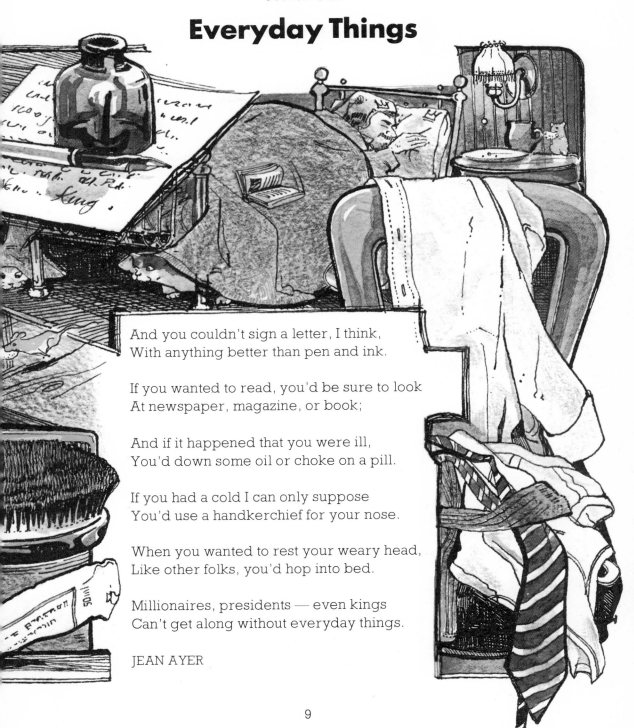

And you couldn't sign a letter, I think,
With anything better than pen and ink.

If you wanted to read, you'd be sure to look
At newspaper, magazine, or book;

And if it happened that you were ill,
You'd down some oil or choke on a pill.

If you had a cold I can only suppose
You'd use a handkerchief for your nose.

When you wanted to rest your weary head,
Like other folks, you'd hop into bed.

Millionaires, presidents — even kings
Can't get along without everyday things.

JEAN AYER

Things Around Us

'I see a long green serpent
With its tail in the dahlias'

The above lines are about something as commonplace as a garden hose. If you read the poems in this section and think about the following questions you might look at these 'everyday things' in a new way.

What familiar things surround you at home?

.... Think of — bubbling pans and boiling kettles .... squashed toothpaste tubes and slippery soap .... school clothes and favourite toys .... old comics and newspapers.

.... Think of — popping toasters .... ringing phones .... noisy vacuum cleaners .... blaring radios and televisions.

If you wish to write your own poem, these words may help you.

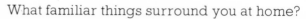

ordinary	fabric	curious	pointed	collect	pattern	construct
utensils	garments	fantastic	blunt	design	style	fashion
equipment	silhouette	sharp	curved	bizarre	model	furniture

In the Fashion

Elizabeth Jennings has written a poem about our clothes.

Write about and draw what people might have worn a hundred years ago and five hundred years ago. Think in particular about rich people, poor people and those who had special uniforms.

Draw some sketches of the sort of clothes you think we may be wearing in a hundred years time.

If you turn to page 15 you will find some questions on the poems themselves and some more things to do.

Clothes

My mother keeps on telling me
When she was in her teens
She wore quite different clothes from mine
And hadn't heard of jeans,

T-shirts, no hats, and dresses that
Reach far above our knees.
I laughed at first and then I thought
One day my kids will tease

And scoff at what *I'm* wearing now.
What will *their* fashions be?
I'd give an awful lot to know,
To look ahead and see.

Girls dressed like girls perhaps once more
And boys no longer half
Resembling us. Oh, what's in store
To make *our* children laugh?

ELIZABETH JENNINGS

Soap

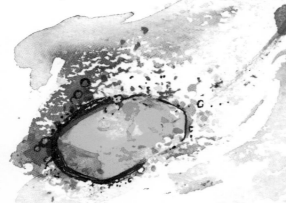

Soap lives in water
And is hard to catch,
Slipping through your fingers
Especially in the bath.

It hasn't a handle to hold
And can't be fastened with string;
It hasn't a zip to close
Or a cardboard box to go in.

It doesn't answer a whistle
Or come for milk or a biscuit;
It won't go into a kennel
Or curl up and sleep in a basket.

Soap is a square slippery fish:
I wish it would stay in its place
And not always vanish
While I'm washing my face.

STANLEY COOK

Letters

Letters are pushed through the flap,
Dive through the air and flop on the mat;
Or sulk inside the letter box,
Annoyed at being trapped;
Or in the morning the postman knocks
And hands your letters in
Before they get up to anything;
Or pushes them under the door
And sends them skidding across the floor.
Letters let people send
Good news and wishes to their friends.
Letters come in trains,
Ships and aeroplanes
From islands in the sea
Where monkeys use the trees
For climbing frames.
Letters come from aunts
With birthday presents;
From a stamp the Queen in her crown
In a brown or purple picture looks down
On your name and address that they wrote
In the middle of the envelope.

Letters come to school
From people who are ill
Saying 'Thank you, children,
For the messages and lovely flowers.'
Letters ask you away
For a fortnight's holiday
With your grandpa and grandmother
When the sun is an oven in summer
Baking your arms and legs
And the bald top
Of grandpa's head
As brown as a crust of bread.
Letters have to be carried,
But they wish they could walk;
And letters have to be read
But they wish they could talk.

STANLEY COOK

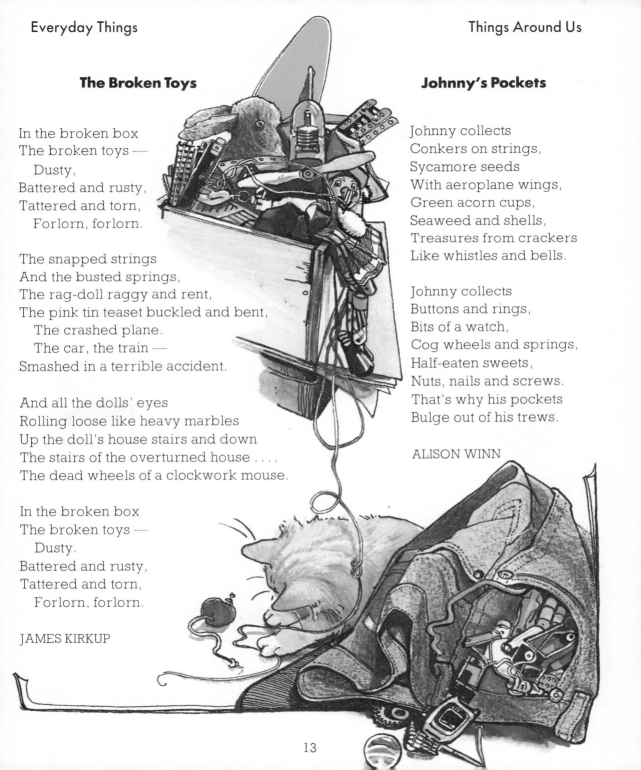

The Broken Toys

In the broken box
The broken toys —
    Dusty,
Battered and rusty,
Tattered and torn,
    Forlorn, forlorn.

The snapped strings
And the busted springs,
The rag-doll raggy and rent,
The pink tin teaset buckled and bent,
    The crashed plane.
    The car, the train —
Smashed in a terrible accident.

And all the dolls' eyes
Rolling loose like heavy marbles
Up the doll's house stairs and down
The stairs of the overturned house . . . .
The dead wheels of a clockwork mouse.

In the broken box
The broken toys —
    Dusty.
Battered and rusty,
Tattered and torn,
    Forlorn, forlorn.

JAMES KIRKUP

Johnny's Pockets

Johnny collects
Conkers on strings,
Sycamore seeds
With aeroplane wings,
Green acorn cups,
Seaweed and shells,
Treasures from crackers
Like whistles and bells.

Johnny collects
Buttons and rings,
Bits of a watch,
Cog wheels and springs,
Half-eaten sweets,
Nuts, nails and screws.
That's why his pockets
Bulge out of his trews.

ALISON WINN

Flashlight

My flashlight tugs me
through the dark
like a hound
with a yellow eye,

sniffs
at the edges
of steep places,

paws
at moles'
and rabbits'
holes,

points its nose
where sharp things
lie asleep —

and then it bounds
ahead of me
on home ground.

JUDITH THURMAN

The Garden Hose

In the grey evening
I see a long green serpent
With its tail in the dahlias

It lies in loops across the grass
And drinks softly at the fawcet

I can hear it swallow

BEATRICE JANOSCO

Poetry Close-up

1. Stanley Cook has written a poem about letters. Why is it that the Queen 'looks down' on your name and address?

2. Several of the poems compare common things to animals. Which animals are mentioned in the poems?

3. How many different things are there in 'Johnny's Pockets'?

4. In the poem 'The Broken Toys' what word does James Kirkup use to tell us that the broken toys are not happy?

5. Beatrice Janosco tells us about 'The Garden Hose' drinking at the fawcet. What is a fawcet?

6. What do you think the 'sharp things' are in Judith Thurman's poem about the 'Flashlight'?

7. Write short descriptions of three common objects without actually naming them. Can your friends guess what they are?

Other Things To Do

1. Find out what your clothes are made of by looking at the labels. Some fabrics are from animals, some are from plants and some are man-made. Find out how the fabrics are manufactured. Which are the most common? Why?

2. Imagine what a house built in a hundred years time would look like. Make some drawings of the different rooms. Describe the furniture and fittings.

Everyday Machines

'And now, if you will set us to our task,
We will serve you four and twenty hours a day!'

In this section you will find some poets' thoughts about things people have invented. Read the poems and think about these questions.

Have you ever stopped to listen to the noise of machines?

.... Think of —silent computers .... chattering typewriters .... thumping generators .... roaring furnaces .... ear-splitting road drills.

Do you find machines interesting or frightening?

.. Think of —a tangle of wires and fuses .... oil and grease .... pulleys, gears and wheels .... relentless conveyor belts .... precision and power.

If you wish to write your own poem these words may help you.

mechanical	deafening	smooth	drive	splutter	energy
lever	fuel	spin	apparatus	motor	intent
clockwork	heat	rattle	create	spring	cog
reverberate	industry	lift	hammer	glide	clank

Inventions

Many of the things we use were invented fairly recently.

Find out as much as you can about these people and about their inventions.

Guglielmo Marconi   Thomas Alva Edison
John Logie Baird   Alexander Graham Bell

If you turn to page 20, you will find some questions on the poems themselves and some more things to do.

THE POETRY LIBRARY

The Toaster

A silver-scaled dragon with jaws flaming red
Sits at my elbow and toasts my bread.
I hand him fat slices, and then, one by one,
He hands them back when he sees they are done.

WILLIAM JAY SMITH

The Vacuum Cleaner

Press a switch with your finger or foot
And the vacuum cleaner gathers a harvest
From the wide field of the carpet
Of yesterday's litter and dust.

Fallen birdseed and bits of grit,
Hairgrips and twisted pins
That bounce and rattle inside it
Make a bagful for the bin.

It finds beneath your feet
A thread of cotton, a cornflake,
A wrapper without a sweet
And the last iced crumb of a cake.

Like a detective looking for clues
It gathers from the floor
Each little thing that proves
What happened the day before.

STANLEY COOK

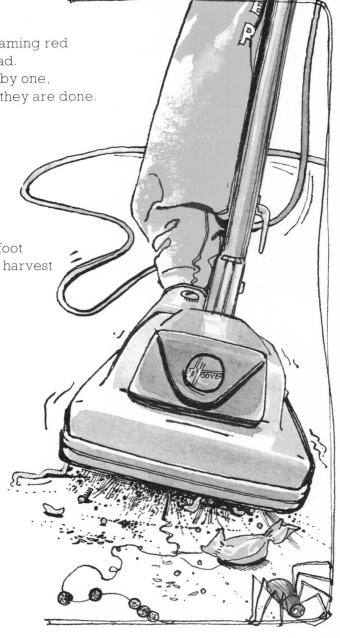

Breakdown

Rackerty clackerty
clickerty BONG
the washing machine
has gone terribly wrong,

It's swallowed a button!
It's stuck in its jaw!
Do you think it will ever
get out any more?

Hark at its spluttering
clickerty-bump —
the washing is churning
all up in a lump,

And just for a button
so shiny and small!
O why did we ever
have buttons at all?

Rackerty clackerty
clickerty clack . . . .
Hooray! THAT sounds better —
the button's come back!

JEAN KENWARD

The Radio Men

When I was little more than six
I thought that men must be
Alive inside the radio
To act in plays or simply blow
Trumpets, or sing to me.

I never got a glimpse of them,
They were so very small.
But I imagined them in there,
Their voices bursting on the air
Through that thin, wooden wall.

ELIZABETH JENNINGS

What Does the Clock Say?

What does the clock say?
Nothing at all.
It hangs all day
and night on the wall
with nothing to say
with nothing to tell
except sometimes
to ting a bell.
And yet it is strange
that the short and the tall
the large, the clever,
the great and the small
will do nothing whatever
nothing at all
without asking it,
the clock on the wall.

GEORGE BARKER

The Guillotine

Obedient to the will of men
The giant blade descends again,
Slicing the molten steel like cheese
Just as the grimy pigmies please:

And something makes me laugh to see
One mass of metal quietly
Slicing another at the will
Of bow-legged Mike and one-eyed Bill.

WILFRID GIBSON

from **The Secret of the Machines**

We were taken from the ore-bed and the mine,
   We were melted in the furnace and the pit—
We were cast and wrought and hammered to design,
   We were cut and filed and tooled and gauged to fit.
Some water, coal, and oil is all we ask,
   And a thousandth of an inch to give us play:
And now, if you will set us to our task,
   We will serve you four and twenty hours a day!

RUDYARD KIPLING

Poetry Close-up

1. Wilfrid Gibson in the poem 'The Guillotine' compares steel to cheese. Why?

   In the same poem who are 'the grimy pigmies'?

2. What does everyone ask 'the clock on the wall' in George Barker's poem?

   Does the clock really say 'Nothing at all'?

   Does the poet feel that the clock is important and if so, why?

3. In which poem are little men supposed to be inside the machine?

4. In the poem 'The Vacuum Cleaner' by Stanley Cook you will find he describes that machine as 'like a detective'. Why might a real detective empty a vacuum cleaner bag?

5. Imagine the newspaper headline

       'Machines take over the World'

   Write the story.

Other Things To Do

1. Look at some of the illustrations of strange machines in any of the 'Professor Branestawm' books by Norman Hunter. Invent your own machine for tying shoelaces and make a detailed drawing of it.

2. Find out how a camera works.

   Why were old silent films so jerky?

3. Find out as much as you can about the industries in your area.

The Town

Wasteland

Rainbow coloured water and rank grass
Stretched for as far as one could see.
The great chimney of the brickworks
Dominated the hills.

Dirty black smoke puffed out,
Discolouring the sky.
The waters, river bed and vegetation
Were rimmed and coated with emerald smelly slime.

Rusty iron and steel frames,
Tin cans, broken chairs and beer bottles
Engulfed the marshland.
Here man's refuse had taken over.

MARK CHAPLIN

Streets in The Town

'The stopping, starting traffic
And the tipper-tap of feet'

In this section you will find some poets' thoughts on the town, its crowds and streets.

Read the poems and think about these questions.

How would you describe a town's busy thoroughfares?

.... Think of —people jostling .... shuffling queues .... impatient shoppers.

.... Think of —dirty pavements .... crumbling stonework .... windswept litter.

.... Think of —pungent fumes .... throbbing engines .... horns blowing .... sirens wailing .... screeching brakes .... the calm at the close of the day.

If you wish to write your own poem, these words may help you.

dust	drab	clamour	puddle	vital	exciting
grey	shabby	clatter	vibrate	lively	umbrellas
danger	decay	tumult	bustle	laden	thriving
loud	dingy	throng	flurry	purposeful	grimy

Beneath Your Feet

Underneath any busy street lies a world we never see, but one which supplies us with services we take for granted. These include gas, electricity and water. Choose one of these services and make your own booklet explaining

a) How it is made or collected;

b) How it is distributed;

c) How it is used.

If you turn to page 27 you will find some questions on the poems themselves and some more things to do.

from **All Along the Street**

The stopping, starting traffic
And the tipper-tap of feet
Weave a tapestry of magic
All along the street.

Here a rich, brown smell of coffee,
There a bakery smell of bread,
Not for sale, but given free;
And they throw in for good measure
The stopping, starting traffic,
And the tipper-tap of feet,
That weave a tapestry of magic
All along the street.

F.J. TESKEY

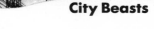

City Beasts

If I were in a jungle dark,
   I wouldn't cross a place
Where I might run into a lion
   Or tiger, face to face.

So in the city I will try
   To do the very same,
For everybody knows that cars
   Are not exactly tame!

I'll wait at corners when I should,
   Watch where I go, and see
That I'm not crossing any trails
   Where city beasts might be.

FRANCES GORMAN RISSER

London Eclogue

The buses trundle,
The trams slide,
Packed on top,
Crammed inside;
The lorries crunch,
The taxis twist;
They pant and bunch
And screech at the lights;
In black rivers,
The walkers pour;
Skies drop darkness,
Walls roar;
Deep tunnels worm,
Great towers rise,
The folk squirm
On a million straps;
In window boxes,
Adam delves;
Infants play
On concrete shelves;
Hither, thither,
Multitudes rush;
The trees wither,
The grass dies;
And the Transport Board,
with a smile seraphic,
Gloats on the growth
of London traffic.

F.J. OSBORN

The Rush Hour

The traffic jam was like a slow-moving snake,
Curling and squirming,
Meandering in and out,
Suddenly starting and stopping,
Never breaking the continuous train.
A gap!
The cars burst forward
Using up every inch of space
Impatient and greedy.

They sound their horns.
The noisy air drowns the whirring of the engines.
The cars are enveloped in a thick black curtain
Of smoke pouring from the exhaust.
Passers-by cough and splutter looking disgustedly

Down at the supposed comforts of man.
The confusion at the head of the snake lessens.
Soon the cars move forward.
The impatience and greediness is gone,
The dark smoky air clears,
And the rush hour is over.

GILLIAN ANDERSON

Preludes 1

The Winter evening settles down
With smells of steaks in passageways.
Six o'clock.
The burnt-out ends of smoky days.
And now a gusty shower wraps
The grimy scraps
Of withered leaves about your feet
And newspapers from vacant lots;
The showers beat
On broken blinds and chimney-pots,
And at the corner of the street
A lonely cab-horse steams and stamps

And then the lighting of the lamps.

T.S. ELIOT

City Lights

Huge round oranges of light
Ripen against the thin dark of the city sky,
Spilling their juice in warm pools
    on bare dry pavements.
Below them blink the traffic lights
    like the eyes of enormous cats
Crouching in the dark —
Crouching and breathing with the heavy
    purr of the traffic.
And winking tail lights slide and dart
    like goldfish
In the pale streams pouring from
    shop windows.

MARGARET GREAVES

Poetry Close-up

1. With what does the poet compare traffic in the poem 'City Beasts'?

2. Read the poem 'City Lights' by Margaret Greaves.

   a) Why do you think she compares the traffic lights to 'the eyes of enormous cats'?

   b) What are the 'pale streams' pouring from the shop windows?

3. Look at the extract from the poem ' All Along the Street'. Why does the poet describe the street as a tapestry of magic?

4. Gillian Anderson's poem 'The Rush Hour' mentions passers-by looking at 'the supposed comforts of man'. Why are they not real comforts?

5. Write a story in which you imagine that you are lost in a busy town.

Other Things To Do

1. Suggest ways of reducing the litter problem in your town.

2. Design a poster which will encourage everyone to keep your school clean and tidy.

3. Explain what graffiti is and why it is a problem.

4. How does a modern street differ from a Victorian street?

5. Find out what the recycling of waste material means.

Places in The Town

'Salford Road, Salford Road,
Is this the place where I was born,'

In this section you will find some poets' thoughts on special places in the town. Read the poems and think about these questions.

Do you enjoy shopping?

.... Think of —crowded stores .... babies crying .... tired legs .... new clothes .... buying presents .... the toy department!

What is it like in a town park?

.... Think of —swings and roundabouts .... boating lakes .... pets' corners .... ball games .... quiet benches .... floral displays.

What is interesting in your nearest town?

.... Think of —busy markets .... museums and libraries .... sports stadiums .... old buildings and modern precincts.

If you wish to write your own poem, these words may help you.

vendor	purchaser	crush	faceless	multi-storey	lift
bridge	variety	dream	friendly	wasteland	jostling
hypermarket	sale	serene	community	warehouse	calm
awning	statue	excited	ancient	arcade	church

Tourist Trail

Imagine that the local council is very keen to attract tourists to your area. You are given the job of producing a visitors' guide.

The guide should make even the worst parts of your town sound attractive and might include:- maps and illustrations, local attractions, places to stay, a good-food guide and local amenities.

If you turn to page 36 you will find some questions on the poems themselves and some more things to do.

Church, School, Park and Shop

Church, school, park, shop,
Traffic jerking, forced to stop;
Slash of green between the stone,
Washing on the lines, well blown.
Smoke rising in slow curl,
Dust-filled air in constant swirl;
Pavements slabbed and kerbed with wear,
Bumped with pram and small push-chair.
Gas-tower green in grimy squat,
Buildings joined in puzzling knot;
Factory site in blackened sprawl,
Waste-filled chimney, wisely tall.
Yards of rubbish, metal wrecks,
Junk in squalor, no-one checks;
Water hidden underground,
Fountain, river, gutter-bound.
Posters, hoardings, hotel signs,
Depot, garage, railway lines;
Somewhere standing midst it all,
Police Station, Post Office — and Old Town Hall.

MARIAN COLLIHOLE

Hump, the Escalator

Hump, the Escalator, slid
Out of the basement — yes, he did!
Out of the basement unawares,
Flattened a moment, then made a stairs;
Made a stairs that moved and crawled
Up through a runway, narrow-walled.

Here I stood on the floor below,
Then on a stair-step rising slow.
Over the heads of the shoppers then —
Dressed-up ladies and bothered men;

Over the aisles of hats and hose —
Over the shelf-displays I rose!
Suddenly stood on the second floor,
Not on a stairway any more.

Every rider ahead of me
Took it stiffly and solemnly.
Nobody paid a penny's fare —
Or knew they had ridden a Magic Stai

ANON.

Going to the Launderette

When my mother goes
To the launderette down the road
She packs a case with clothes
As if we were going away
For an hour's holiday.

While the clothes are washing clean
Twisting like snakes in the machine
She sits with her friends on the row of seats
Or helps them stretch and fold their sheets.

I watch through the glass of the drier door
The cloth snakes climb up the curving wall
Until it stops and back they fall
Tired with trying to its floor.

STANLEY COOK

The Park

In the middle of the city
Is an open space called a Park;
It is difficult for us to do what we like there
Even after dark.

In the middle of the Park there is a statue,
A huge man made of stone;
We are not allowed to climb his legs or scribble on
    his trousers,
He has to be left alone.

In the middle of the grass there is some water
Surrounded by an asphalt path;
We are forbidden to fish or throw stones into it
Or swim or take a bath.

In the middle of the water is an island
Full of mysterious things,
But none of us has ever set foot upon it
Because none of us has wings.

OLIVE DEHN

Carbreakers

There's a graveyard in our street,
But it's not for putting people in;
The bodies that they bury here
Are made of steel and paint and tin.

The people come and leave their wrecks
For crunching in the giant jaws
Of a great hungry car-machine,
That lives on bonnets, wheels and doors.

When I pass by the yard at night,
I sometimes think I hear a sound
Of ghostly horns that moan and whine,
Upon that metal-graveyard mound.

MARIAN LINES

Summer Night at Hyde Park Corner

Great globes of light spill yellow rain:
    Pencils of gold through purple gloom.
The buses swarm like heavy bees
    Trailing fat bodies. Faces loom,
Moonlike, and fade away among the trees
    Which, lit beneath by lamplight, bloom
High in darkness. Distant traffic
    Sounds with dull, enclosing boom . . . .

Sleep extends a velvet forepaw.
    Night spreads out a downsoft plume.

A.S.J. TESSIMOND

Pushcart Row

In rain or shine; in heat or snow;
The pushcarts stretch in a long green row,
Close to the curb as they can crowd,
With men all shouting their wares aloud.
If you have need of a lettuce head,
Or a bunch of radishes shiny red,
Of onions, carrots, or cauliflower,
Oranges sweet or lemons sour,
Polished apples or dripping greens,
Fat little mushrooms, thin string beans.
Of fruits and berries plump and round,
By the basket, by the pound —
Bring out your purse and take your pick
Where the two-wheeled pushcarts cluster thick;
Where dogs and children play about
Wheels and pavement and gutter-spout;
Where the women wear shawls and earrings gold
And the men are mostly brown and old
With selling their wares in shine or snow
On the cobblestones of Pushcart Row.

RACHEL FIELD

Salford Road

Salford Road, Salford Road,
Is this the place where I was born,
With a green front gate, a red brick wall
And hydrangeas round a lawn.

Salford Road, Salford Road,
Is the road where we would play
Where the sky lay over the roof tops
Like a friend who'd come to stay.

The Gardeners lived at fifty-five,
The Lunds with the willow tree,
Mr Pool with the flag and the garden pond
And the Harndens at fifty-three.

There was riding bikes and laughing
Till we couldn't laugh any more,
And bilberries picked on the hillside
And picnics on the shore.

I lay in bed when I was four
As the sunlight turned to grey
And heard the train through my pillow
And the seagulls far away.

And I rose to look out of my window
For I knew that someone was there
And a man stood as sad as nevermore
And didn't see me there.

And when I stand in Salford Road
And think of the boy who was me
I feel that from one of the windows
Someone is looking at me.

My friends walked out one Summer day,
Walked singing down the lane,
My friends walked into a wood called Time
And never came out again.

We live in a land called Gone-Today
That's made of bricks and straw
But Salford Road runs through my head
To a land called Evermore.

GARETH OWEN

Poetry Close-up

1. Make a list of the things sold on 'Pushcart Row'.

2. What rules are there in 'The Park' described by Olive Dehn?

3. In the poem 'Summer Night at Hyde Park Corner':
   a) What makes the rain look yellow?
   b) Why does the poet compare buses to heavy bees?

4. Look at the poem 'Hump, the Escalator'. How does the poet make the escalator seem like an animal?

5. Read the poem 'Salford Road'. Is this a sad or a happy poem? Why?

6. Write a story in which you imagine you are an old Rolls Royce car reminiscing about your life.

Other Things To Do

1. Design an advertisement for a new product you are going to introduce into shops.

2. Make a detailed survey of the shops and buildings in the main street of your town. With the help of a graph, show how many different types there are.

3. Find out about each of these shops: pawnbroker, pharmacist, herbalist, confectioner, cobbler and florist.

4. Write a few lines about the jobs of these people: accountant, bank manager, solicitor, estate agent and insurance broker.

Buildings and Structures

Change

Those flats that once were fields,
Cut up by the knife that man wields,
The knife made of bulldozers, picks, shovels and a
    crane —
The noise is enough to make you insane.
I really don't know how men can endure
The rubbish and muck that smells like a sewer,
But life goes on, you take a breath
Of the gas they call air, and you feel like death itself.

Over there (he points to a nuclear station,
Which now is a shrine to vast automation)
Was a beautiful farm.
If they'd left it alone, it wouldn't have done any harm.
In winter, the fields were covered with snow,
You could see the winter sun aglow,
Then the snow would turn to sleet.
But now the fields are a grave of concrete.
Oh, my God, what have they done to this place?
What is happening to my human race?

NICK GODWIN

Building

'To build a house you need a painted hut
You bring to the site on the back of a lorry'

This is one child's idea of what is needed to build a house.

Perhaps a little more is necessary!

Read the poems and think about these questions.

How are houses built?

Think of — a muddy site .... bulldozers and diggers .... piles of bricks .... rumbling mixers .... scaffolding and rising walls .... joiners, glaziers and painters .... new owners.

What finally happens to all buildings?

.... Think of — empty shells .... crashing masonry .... clouds of dust .... smouldering debris .... level ground.

If you wish to write your own poem, these words might help you.

foundation	mortar	beam	rubble	excavate	erect
surveyor	ladders	hod	toil	estate	plaster
throb	vibrate	timber	hammer	plank	fragment
electricians	raze	demolish	site	pipes	cable

Making Plans

Before any building work starts, a plan has to be drawn. A plan is a drawing of an object as if seen from above.

.... Place three small objects on your desk and draw a plan of them.

.... Draw a plan of your class-room, putting in all the furniture and fixtures.

If you turn to page 44 you will find some questions on the poems themselves and some more things to do.

How to Build a House

To build a house you need a painted hut
You bring to the site on the back of a lorry
And other men to help you put it up.

To build a house you need to drink your tea
In the painted hut when the whistle blows
And twiddle your mug to empty the leaves.

To build a house you need to dirty your clothes,
Wear a yellow helmet or a big-peaked cap
And use a coloured handkerchief to blow your nose.

To build a house when the weather is hot
You need a check shirt to take off
And a belt with a buckle round your trouser-top.

To build a house you need to be strong enough
To dig foundations out to start the wall
And climb a ladder after it as it rises up.

To build a house you need to know all
The people who pass and shout to them 'Hello, Jack!
And 'Hello' to me, although I'm still small.

STANLEY COOK

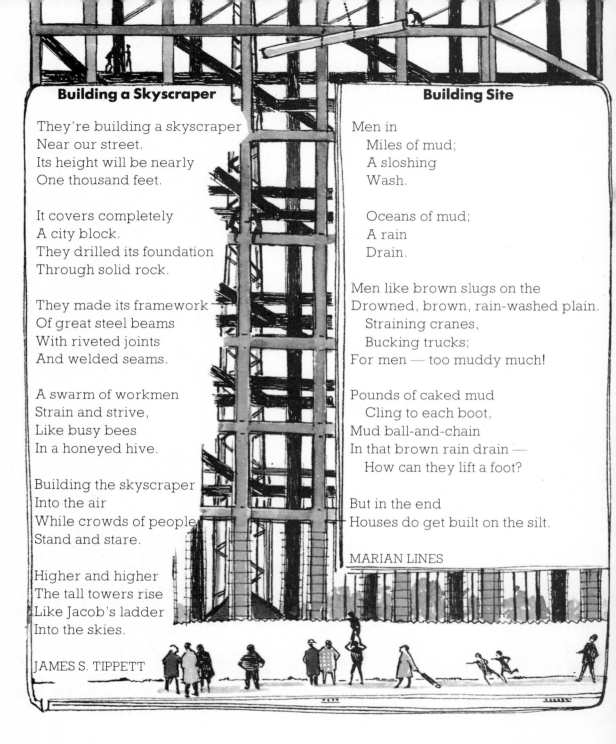

Building a Skyscraper

They're building a skyscraper
Near our street.
Its height will be nearly
One thousand feet.

It covers completely
A city block.
They drilled its foundation
Through solid rock.

They made its framework
Of great steel beams
With riveted joints
And welded seams.

A swarm of workmen
Strain and strive,
Like busy bees
In a honeyed hive.

Building the skyscraper
Into the air
While crowds of people
Stand and stare.

Higher and higher
The tall towers rise
Like Jacob's ladder
Into the skies.

JAMES S. TIPPETT

Building Site

Men in
    Miles of mud;
    A sloshing
    Wash.

    Oceans of mud;
    A rain
    Drain.

Men like brown slugs on the
Drowned, brown, rain-washed plain.
    Straining cranes,
    Bucking trucks;
For men — too muddy much!

Pounds of caked mud
    Cling to each boot,
Mud ball-and-chain
In that brown rain drain —
    How can they lift a foot?

But in the end
Houses do get built on the silt.

MARIAN LINES

The Excavator

Here she comes again,
For another load;
Jerking over ruts and bumps
On the rough ground of
The building site.
The caterpillar wheels,
Ribbed,
Roll over to the heap of rubble.

Strong, powerful, unwieldy,
Yet useful.
She brakes, stops,
And with the pull of one lever
The huge machine begins
To work.
Smoothly,
The excavator lowers its jib.
Thick grease is revealed
As the piston opens.
A snort,
And the shovel has begun its meal.
Digging into clay and stones;
The teeth make mince-meat of the rock.
A push, a pull,
And the mouth is full.
Retracting,
And not letting a spoonful go,
She rises
Majestically;
And she has succeeded.
Then, as expected,
Has eaten too much,
And is sick
Into the lorry.

N. MANTON

Steam Shovel

The dinosaurs are not all dead.
I saw one raise its iron head
To watch me walking down the road
Beyond our house today.
Its jaws were dripping with a load
Of earth and grass that it had cropped.
It must have heard me where I stopped.
Snorted white steam my way,
And stretched its long neck out to see,
And chewed, and grinned quite amiably.

CHARLES MALAM

The Cement Mixer

Eating sand, stones and water, he turns his great mouth,
Making cement.
He dips his mouth and pours cement into a wheelbarrow.
He eats all day long.
He has no manners —
Standing eating all day long.

HUGH EVA

Demolition of a Crescent

Families gone,
Boards in the windows,
Houses alone,
Waiting the end.
Ruin is near,
Street in its death-throes;
Leaving a scar
No one can mend.

    Swing the hammer!
    Fell the trees!
    Bring the Crescent to its knees!

See where they fall,
Lintel and staircase.
Batter them all
Flat to the ground!
Chimneystacks tumbled,
Skylight and fireplace,
Houses are humbled, —
Crescent is down.

    Swing the hammer!
    Fell the trees!
    Bring the Crescent to its knees!

MARIAN LINES

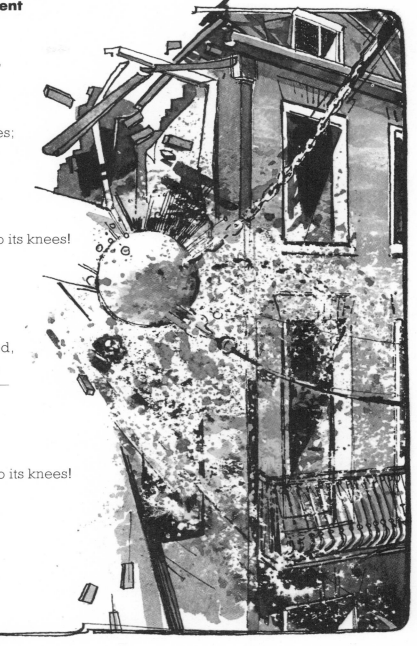

Poetry Close-up

1. List the parts of a building you can find in Marian Lines' poem 'Demolition of a Crescent'.

2. Read 'The Excavator' by N. Manton and 'The Cement Mixer' by Hugh Eva. With what do the poets compare the machines' actions? Can you write down some phrases and words from the poems to support your ideas?

3. How are the workmen like bees and the building like a hive in James Tippett's poem 'Building a Skyscraper'?

   In the same poem, find out what 'Jacob's ladder' was, and why the poet uses that phrase.

4. Why does Marian Lines describe the men as 'like brown slugs' in her poem 'Building Site'?

5. In 'How to Build a House' by Stanley Cook, how can you tell that the poem is supposed to be written by a child?

6. Imagine that you are a brick in a building. Try to describe your life from the moment you left the ground as a lump of clay.

Other Things To Do

1. Find out about the famous architect Sir Christopher Wren. Write about his life and draw some of the buildings he planned. Can you find out about any other well-known architects?

2. Make a topic book about famous buildings. These are some you could include:-
   Taj Mahal . . . . Leaning Tower of Pisa . . . . The Pyramids . . . . Eiffel Tower . . . . Empire State Building.

3. Design a stained-glass window.

Structures

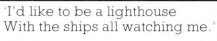

'I'd like to be a lighthouse
With the ships all watching me.'

In this section you will find some poems about different structures. Read the poems and then think about these questions on the world we have made.

What 'furniture' is there in your street?

.... Think of —black grids .... squat pillar-boxes ....
bright telephone kiosks .... fading
signs .... lines of telegraph poles.

What large structures are there near you?

.... Think of —high viaducts .... dark tunnels ....
sprawling factories .... stark pylons
.... floodlit stadiums.

What sort of materials are used in man-made structures?

.... Think of —gleaming steel and rusty iron .... solid
concrete and fragile glass .... pitted
brick and painted wood.

If you wish to write your own poem, these words may help you.

corrugated	girder	crumble	cracked	stainless	angular
transparent	aluminium	brass	smoky	rigid	sturdy
grime	support	neon	functional	graceful	eyesore
bleak	ornate	tarnished	wrought	forged	copper

Mysterious Monuments

Stonehenge was built thousands of years ago and archaeologists are still unsure of its purpose.

Find out where it is .... where the stone came from .... the possible methods used to build it.

Why do you think it was built? Do you know of any other mysterious structures?

If you turn to page 50 you will find some questions on the poems themselves and some more things to do.

Piers

I am fond of piers
rather as I am
of large ungainly friendly animals.

Look at this one
on its spindly legs
lurching out
over the chocolate mud,
to dabble all its barnacled old feet
into the salty water at low tide.

I should be sad if piers became extinct
like other animals
I've heard about.

DOUGLAS GIBSON

I'd Like to be a Lighthouse

I'd like to be a lighthouse
   All scrubbed and painted white.
I'd like to be a lighthouse
   And stay awake all night
To keep my eye on everything
   That sails my patch of sea;
I'd like to be a lighthouse
   With the ships all watching me.

RACHEL FIELD

The World of Hoardings

Twenty feet tall he stands.
He could tear up a house with his hands.
His smile is a cheerful yard,
His arms are immense, and hard.
He's a giant, a giant, a giant from the world of Hoardings.

His bottle of milk holds so much
That if it spilled at his touch
In a torrent of milk we'd drown!
White milk would flood the town!
It's a giant, a giant, a giant from the world of Hoardings.

There, words are roof-top high.
Black and red, they yell at the sky
With a gusty, bellowing voice,
And they *look* like the storm-wide voice
Of a giant, a giant, a giant from the world of Hoardings.

But if we duck under this board
We can see, without looking too hard,
That they're all paper-thin,
And pasted on panels of tin,
Those giants, those giants, giants from the world of Hoardings.

LESLIE NORRIS

The Statue

On a stone chair in the market-place
Sits a stone gentleman with a stone face.
He is great, he is good, he is old as old —
How many years I've not been told.
Great things he did a great while ago,
And what they were I do not know.
But solemn and sad is his great square face
As he sits high up on his square stone base.
Day after day he sits just so,
With some words in a foreign tongue below.
Whether the wind blows warm or cold,
His stone clothes alter never a fold.
One stone hand he rests on his knee;
With the other stone hand he points at me.
Oh, why does he look at me in just that way?
I'm afraid to go, and afraid to stay:
Stone gentleman, what have you got to say?

JAMES REEVES

There's a Red Brick Wall

There's a red brick wall
    along our street
that stands and burns
    in the sun's hot heat.

There aren't any flames
    but I know it burns.
When I walk by,
    it glows and turns
    my face to fire.

NANCY CHAMBERS

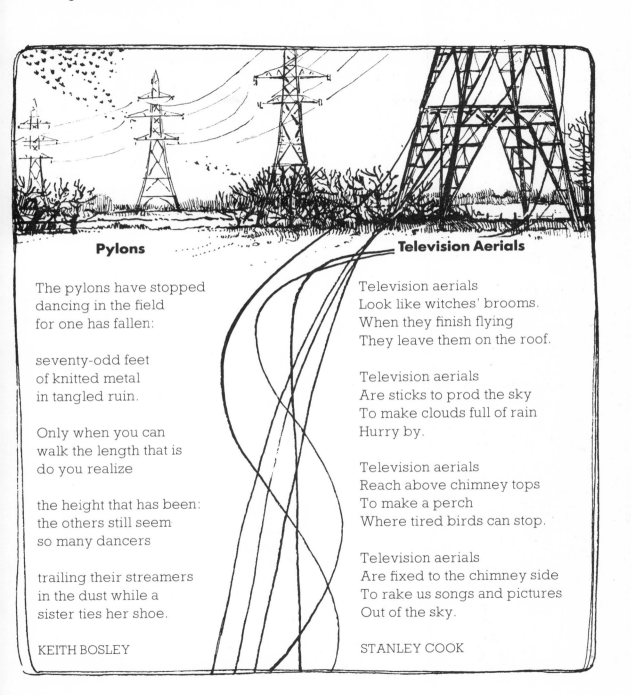

Pylons

The pylons have stopped
dancing in the field
for one has fallen:

seventy-odd feet
of knitted metal
in tangled ruin.

Only when you can
walk the length that is
do you realize

the height that has been:
the others still seem
so many dancers

trailing their streamers
in the dust while a
sister ties her shoe.

KEITH BOSLEY

Television Aerials

Television aerials
Look like witches' brooms.
When they finish flying
They leave them on the roof.

Television aerials
Are sticks to prod the sky
To make clouds full of rain
Hurry by.

Television aerials
Reach above chimney tops
To make a perch
Where tired birds can stop.

Television aerials
Are fixed to the chimney side
To rake us songs and pictures
Out of the sky.

STANLEY COOK

Poetry Close-up

1. In 'There's a Red Brick Wall' by Nancy Chambers, why does the wall burn you?

2. Why does the lighthouse stay awake all night in Rachel Field's poem 'I'd Like to be a Lighthouse'?

3. Write the words Douglas Gibson uses in his poem to compare an animal to the pier.

4. Keith Bosley talks about dancers, streamers and a sister tying her shoelace in the last two verses of 'Pylons'. Can you explain what he means by these phrases?

5. What do you think James Reeves feels about 'The Statue'?

6. Who is the giant in 'The World of Hoardings' by Leslie Norris?

   Imagine that everything did come to life from 'The World of Hoardings'. Describe what happened. How could everything be restored to normal?

Other Things To Do

1. Find out which seaside resorts still have piers and show them on your own map of Britain. On the same map mark on some well-known lighthouses.

2. What do the numbers on a fire hydrant sign mean?

3. What information can you find on your local post-box? Are there any clues as to how old it is?

A Place to Live

'And yet to the postman it's only a number'.

Our homes are very special to us. Read these poems about places to live and then think about these questions.

What makes your house a home?

.... Think of —a welcoming light .... an opening door .... familiar faces .... mum's cooking .... your own bed.

Are empty houses exciting?

.... Think of —overgrown gardens .... gaping roofs .... cracked windows .... creaking doors .... strange noises.

Are all homes the same?

.... Think of —bungalows and multi-storeyed flats .... double glazing and leaded windows .... slates and thatched roofs .... trim hedges and broken fences.

If you wish to write your own poem, these words may help you.

dwelling	gutter	terrace	deserted	detached	cheerful
dingy	porch	peeling	comfortable	abandoned	snug
neat	shabby	vacant	neglected	views	grimy
panes	drain-pipe	homely	picturesque	faded	spacious

House Warming

A home needs a lot of fuel to keep it warm. The less fuel you use the less it costs! These are some energy-saving ideas.

double glazing	solar-heating panels
thermostats	loft insulation
cavity-wall insulation	draught proofing

Describe how each of these works.

If you turn to page 58 you will find some questions on the poems themselves and some more things to do.

Portrait of a House

The house that we live in was built in a place
That was once a mere cube of unoccupied space;
And the birds that flew through it and passed on their way
Would collide with a wall or a window today.

The rooms in the house are of medium size,
The sort that an ant would regard with surprise;
While a whale could express no opinion at all,
For his bulk would prevent him from passing the hall.

The stairs are arranged with such exquisite skill
That a person can climb or descend them at will;
And the absence of rain from the attics is proof
That the architect thought of supplying a roof.

Of the doors and the windows our only complaint
Is the fact that you can't see the wood for the paint:
A trouble with which we've decided to deal
By allowing the paint to continue to peel.

The chairs and the tables are perfectly tame,
And to speak of them harshly is rather a shame;
But nevertheless I am bound to remark
On their savage resistance when bumped in the dark.

In the kitchen, in spite of its tropical clime,
Two cats and a cook spend the whole of their time.
The cats have been known to meander about,
But the cook is a fixture and never goes out.

It is said that mysterious sounds may be heard
In the house when it's empty; but this is absurd.
If you've gone there to listen, it's clear to a dunce
That the house will have ceased to be empty at once.

We've a spare-room prepared for the casual guest,
But it really is not what the name would suggest;
For although it's a room, it is never to spare,
As someone or other is constantly there.

I have made it quite clear that our chosen abode
Is different from all of the rest in the road —
What a beautiful house for play, dinner and slumber!
And yet to the postman it's only a number.

E.V. RIEU

THE POETRY LIBRARY

Sad . . . and Glad

The sun has gone down,
Leaving an empty sky
  Above the hills
  Above our town.
Street-lamps switch on.
  Buses swish by.
Strangers are laughing.
My friends have gone in:
    I'm alone —
  It's time to go home.

Someone runs to the post,
  Leaving an open door —
    A family
  Makes itself toast
    Round the fire
  Down a long corridor.
    It's chilly,
And I've been out all day:
    I want my tea.
  It's time I was home.

They're calling in Tommy
  (I wish he was me);
  On the allotments
  Bonfire smoke rolls
  Sluggish, blue-grey.
  I'm still streets away:
    This time of year,
    This time of day,
      Makes me sad
  And glad — to get home.

BRIAN LEE

from **Empty House**

There is nothing
Quite so dismal
As an empty house;
The door bell's clangour
Tears apart the silence
Rousing no one.
Nothing moves;
Not a sound
Save the chasing echoes
And the clocks hollow
Tock, tock
Measuring the emptiness;
Behind the frosted door
No friendly, welcome shadow looms,
No footsteps cross the floor.

GARETH OWEN

The Sounds in the Evening

The sounds in the evening
Go all through the house,
The click of the clock
And the pick of the mouse,
The footsteps of people
Upon the top floor,
The skirts of my mother
That brush by the door,
The crick in the boards,
And the creak of the chairs,
The fluttering murmurs
Outside on the stairs,
The ring of the bell,
The arrival of guests,
The laugh of my father
At one of his jests,
The clashing of dishes
As dinner goes in,
The babble of voices
That distance makes thin,
The mewings of cats
That seem just by my ear,
The hooting of owls
That can never seem near,
The queer little noises
That no one explains . . . .
Till the moon through the slats
Of my window-blind rains,
And the world of my eyes
And my ears melts like steam
As I find in my pillow
The world of my dream.

ELEANOR FARJEON

Looking Down on Roofs

When I lived in a basement,
The house above my head
Was like a mountain of brick and wood,
A place of weight and dread.
But now I'm in a Tower Block
I can look right down my nose
At the mingy, stingy streets below,
That lie beneath my toes.

When I lived in a basement,
I smelled the damp all night;
And the cats and rats of the neighbourhood
Would choose our yard to fight.
But now I'm in a Tower Block,
It's clean, and fresh, and high,
And I love to look down on the roofs and know
That I'm nearer to the sky.

MARIAN LINES

Empty House

In the raggle-taggle garden
   Where the thistles grow tall
And brambles clutch
   At the crumbling wall

A raggle-taggle willow-tree
   Leans and sighs
By an empty house
   With sad, dark eyes;

Nettles besiege
   The kitchen door,
And bindweed creeps up
   Through the rotting floor.

Nobody passing
   Looks at it twice;
But the sad old house
   With its blank, dark eyes
   And its raggle-taggle garden
   Is paradise
   For mice!

S. GILMAN

House

The ruins of an old house stand
Without a roof, on muddy land,
Each window is a sightless eye
Staring at the city sky.

Locks are broken, every wall
Looks as if about to fall.
The people who lived here, they say,
Just packed up and went away.

And once when I was playing there
Halfway up the curving stair
I thought I heard a laughing sound
Coming from the trampled ground.

LEONARD CLARK

Houses

I like old houses best, don't you?
They never go cluttering up a view
With roofs too red and paint too new,
With doors too green and blinds too blue!
The old ones look as if they *grew*,
Their bricks may be dingy, their clapboards askew
From sitting so many seasons through,
But they've learned in a hundred years or two
Not to go cluttering up a view!

RACHEL FIELD

Poetry Close-up

1. What different noises does Eleanor Farjeon write about in her poem 'The Sounds in the Evening'?

2. Why would S. Gilman's 'Empty House' be a paradise for mice?

3. How do new houses clutter up the view, according to Rachel Field in her poem 'Houses'?

4. In Leonard Clark's poem 'House', what do you think the laughing sound is, and why does he hear it?

5. a) In 'Empty House' by Gareth Owen, is there anybody living in the house?
    b) In the same poem, what is a frosted door?

6. Why does the poet wish he was Tommy in 'Sad . . . . and Glad'?

7. Describe the sort of house you would like to live in.

Other Things To Do

1. What were teepees and igloos? Who lived in them, how were they built and what were they like inside?

2. What is a Building Society? Find out the address of a local building society and write to it asking for information about its history and business.

3. If you were shipwrecked on a deserted South Sea island, describe how you would build yourself a home.

Travelling

Where?

Where do all the buses go from the end of the street?
And where has that aeroplane come from, where?
What is it like at the end of the line?
How long would it take me to get there?

Is it the same there as here?
Are the schoolteachers kind,
Do policemen not mind
When you ask them to tell you the time?
And if you get lost do the folk lend a hand,
Or do they stare down
With a cold distant frown
And jeer, in a language you can't understand?

Where does the path end, going through the dark wood?
Where do the trains come from that pass in the night?
Where does the road end that starts in our street
If you turn to the left, or the right?
Is it weird there or wonderful; forlorn, busy or queer —
Or ordinary, just like it is here?

BRIAN LEE

By Road

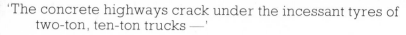

'The concrete highways crack under the incessant tyres of
  two-ton, ten-ton trucks —'

Here are some poets' thoughts on road transport.
Read the poems and then think about these questions.

What kind of vehicles use our roads?

.... Think of —purring limousines and rattling old
bangers .... cumbersome lorries and
nippy vans .... crowded buses and
solitary cycles .... horse-drawn carts
and thundering juggernauts.

What problems do vehicles create?

.... Think of —deafening noise .... frustrating delays
.... choking fumes .... fatal collisions.

What kind of roads do we use?

.... Think of —winding lanes and fast motorways ....
busy streets and suburban avenues.

If you wish to write your own poem, these words may help you.

rumble	kerb	engine	pedestrian	judder	crash
traffic	snarling	highway	hurtle	gradient	driver
load	accelerate	arterial	ribbon	powerful	distance
siren	throbbing	passenger	articulated	route	lumbering

Motorways

.... Today's motorways make long distance journeys much easier. Draw or
trace a map of Britain and mark on it these motorways: M1; M6; M5; M4; M8; M62.
On your map, show the main towns and cities these motorways link.

.... Can you make a list of special traffic rules which apply to motorway users?

If you turn to page 66 you will find some questions on the poems themselves and
some more things to do.

The Bus

Beneath its cover
The engine turns over
Sounding loud and hot
As it waits at the stop,
Thudding like feet
Or a drum-beat.
People push
Onto the bus.
Women in hats,
Men in caps,
Boys in shirts
And girls in skirts,
With hair cut long.
Mothers help
Small children on.

With thank you's and please's
The conductor squeezes
To take the fares.
'One and two halves
And one for him downstairs.'
'Into town'
And 'all the way'.
'I've lost my purse
And I can't pay.'
'I've dropped my money
Under the seat.
See if it's rolled
Beneath your feet.'
'One for me
And one for the dog.

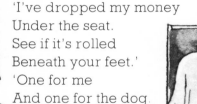

In the sun, rain,
Snow and fog,
In the day
And in the dark,
Past people at windows
And trees in the park,
No time to stop
For sweets in shops,
Picking up
And putting down
The doubledecker
Goes into town.

STANLEY COOK

Motor Cars

From city window, 'way up high,
I like to watch the cars go by.
They look like burnished beetles, black,
That leave a little muddy track
Behind them as they slowly crawl.
Sometimes they do not move at all
But huddle close with hum and drone
As though they feared to be alone.
They grope their way through fog and night
With the golden feelers of their light.

ROWENA BASTIN BENNETT

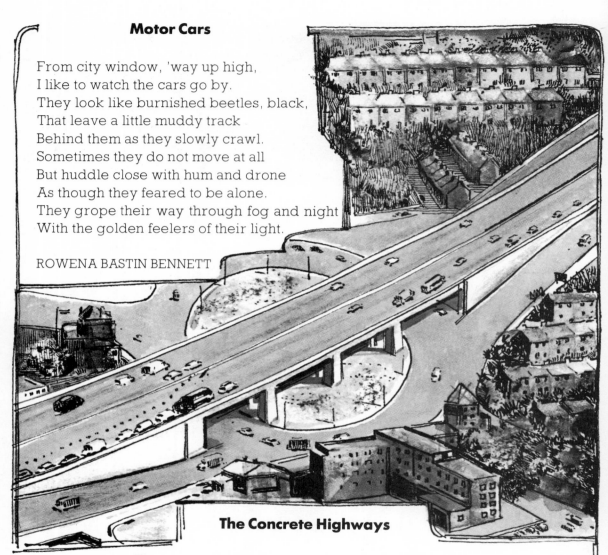

The Concrete Highways

The concrete highways crack under the incessant tyres of
two-ton, ten-ton trucks — and the concrete mixers come
with laughing bellies filled with gravel for the repair jobs.

CARL SANDBURG

The Traffic Light

HALT! My eye is red!
Rolls-Royce, Fiat, Ford,
Halt there, I said.
Down the obedient road,
Brute engines muted,
The meek traffic stands in line
Awaiting my eye of green.

For I command them all!
By day and quiet night
Aloof I stand, and tall,
Banded in black and white.
I am all-powerful.
With one flick of my eye,
It is I who will let them by.

But first, a touch of amber,
A cautious warning.
Now hear the engines roar,
The gears groaning.
Green! Like a stream they pour
Into the city's maze,
On their mysterious ways.

I stand on my one toe
Unable to turn my head.
Oh, how I'd love to know,
As past they speed,
Where they all go.
HALT! My eye is red!
Halt there, I said.

But quite soon I'll let you go.

LESLIE NORRIS

The Road

So you thought the road was tidied
Only on a windy day
That blows up the paper bags
And rolls the empty tins away?

On days as still as a statue
Roads, like clothes and hair, are brushed
And the lorry sprinkles water
To lay the sandy dust.

In Autumn a fat yellow lorry
Like an elephant on wheels
Vacuum cleans the gutters
Of drifts of fallen leaves;

Or, held by a telescopic arm
That reaches up and out,
A man with a woodman's saw
Cuts overhanging branches down.

So you mustn't think
The downtrodden road's only hope
Of a freshening-up is a shower
Of rain without soap.

STANLEY COOK

The Way Through the Woods

They shut the road through the woods
Seventy years ago.
Weather and rain have undone it again,
And now you would never know
There was once a road through the woods
Before they planted the trees.
It is underneath the coppice and heath,
And the thin anemones.
Only the keeper sees
That, where the ring-dove broods,
And the badgers roll at ease,
There was once a road through the woods.

Yet, if you enter the woods
Of a summer evening late,
When the night-air cools on the trout-ringed pools
Where the otter whistles his mate
(They fear not men in the woods,
Because they see so few),
You will hear the beat of a horse's feet,
And the swish of a skirt in the dew,
Steadily cantering through
The misty solitudes,
As though they perfectly knew
The old lost road through the woods . . . .
But there is no road through the woods!

RUDYARD KIPLING

The Old Coach Road

There's hardly a wheel rut left to show
The way the coach road used to go.
Trees straddle it and berries grow
Where coaches rumbled long ago,
And horses' hoofs struck sparks of light,
Many a frosty winter night.
Here gypsy faces, lean and tan,
Peered from some lumbering caravan,
Or pedlars passed with bulging packs
And sheep with sun aslant their backs.
Now, only berry pickers push
Their way through thorn and elder bush —
But sometimes of a night, they say,
Wheels have been heard to pass that way.

RACHEL FIELD

Poetry Close-up

1. Why are the cars in Rowena Bastin Bennett's poem likened to beetles?

2. Who were the different travellers who used 'The Old Coach Road'?

3. In Carl Sandburg's 'The Concrete Highways' can you explain why he thinks the mixers are laughing?

4. From the poem 'The Traffic Light', describe what the traffic does at each colour of the lights.

5. What are the problems the conductor meets in Stanley Cook's poem 'The Bus'?

6. Write a story called 'Suddenly the brakes failed'.

Other Things To Do

1. Read the parts of the Highway Code about pedestrians and cyclists. Then make up a quiz for your friends to answer.

2. Design a poster to explain how a pelican crossing should be used.

3. Draw and write about our roads and vehicles of 200 years ago.

4. Most cars are driven by petrol. Petrol comes from oil. Show the regions where oil is found on a world map. What other products are made from oil?

By Rail

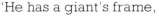

'He has a giant's frame,
He weighs ten thousand pounds of blackness.'

In this section you will find some poets' thoughts
on trains. Read the poems and think about the
following questions on these mechanical giants.

What is it like to be at a busy main-line station?

.... Think of —piles of luggage .... piercing whistles
.... garbled announcements ....
excited children, bored commuters,
flustered grannies .... slamming
doors .... throbbing diesels.

Do you enjoy travelling by train?

.... Think of —swaying coaches .... clattering
rhythm .... unexplained stops ....
sudden tunnels .... scenery flashing by.

Why are steam-engines so exciting?

.... Think of —looming iron monsters .... the shriek
of steam .... grinding metal ....
pounding wheels .... a fiery beast of
the night.

If you wish to write your own poem, these words may help you.

clanking	passengers	clock	tracks	freight	electric
furnace	scream	greetings	farewells	diesel	inter-city
platform	points	buffet	creak	shunt	ticket
buffers	porter	funnel	signal	whistle	siding

On The Tracks

.... The 'Rocket' was one of the most famous steam-
engines.
Draw a picture of this locomotive.
Write about the competition it won in 1877 and
find out about its inventor.

If you turn to page 75 you will find some questions
on the poems themselves and some more things to do.

The Song of the Engine

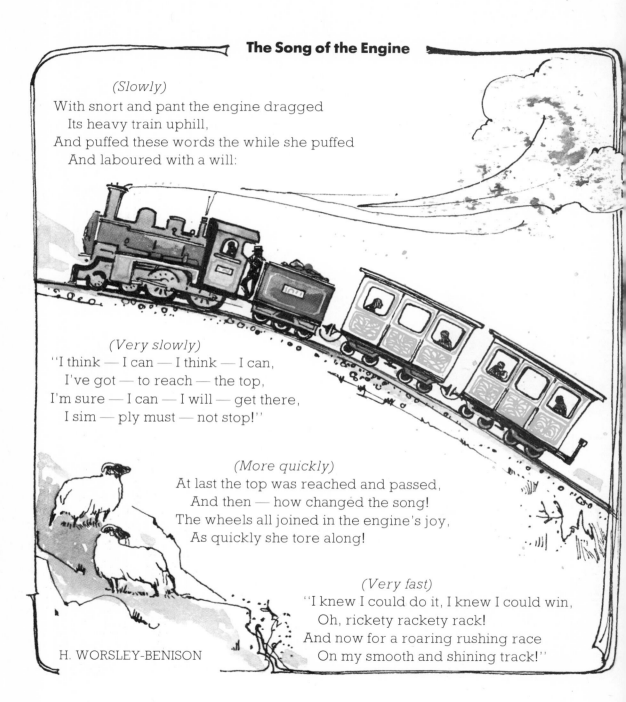

(Slowly)
With snort and pant the engine dragged
　Its heavy train uphill,
And puffed these words the while she puffed
　And laboured with a will:

(Very slowly)
"I think — I can — I think — I can,
　I've got — to reach — the top,
I'm sure — I can — I will — get there,
　I sim — ply must — not stop!"

(More quickly)
At last the top was reached and passed,
　And then — how changed the song!
The wheels all joined in the engine's joy,
　As quickly she tore along!

(Very fast)
"I knew I could do it, I knew I could win,
　Oh, rickety rackety rack!
And now for a roaring rushing race
　On my smooth and shining track!"

H. WORSLEY-BENISON

Puffing Billy

Oh the grand approach at Euston
And the hazards that await!
In a fever of excitement
Show your ticket at the gate;
Then a carriage without harness
And a platform like a quay
And a piston in a system
Of bizarre machinery!

There's one man shovels fuel
While another turns a knob,
Then the boiler starts to sizzle
Like a kettle on the hob,
And we glide demurely forward
With a creak of bolts and nuts,
All the windows full of faces,
All the faces full of smuts.

Then considerably over
Twenty frantic miles an hour
We're preceded by an oven
With a funnel coughing fire.
And no wonder the spectators
Often register complaint,
For the pace is diabolic
And the gentlewomen faint.

It's goodbye to horse and carriage,
Locomotion marches on,
Dick the highwayman turns honest
For his occupation's gone.
Steady, driver, steady,
Or there's bound to be a spill!
Why, bless my soul already
We're at Harrow-on-the-Hill.

CHRISTOPHER HASSALL

Locomotive

He has a giant's frame,
He weighs ten thousand pounds of blackness,
His body is measured out .... his every inch,
His pipes and wheels and countless nuts and bolts are
    rubbed and polished inside and out.
When he moves
The hands of meters are quick to turn;
When he runs
The rails and the sleepers shake;
And when his piston-arms begin to stretch,
When they shuffle to and fro and spin the wheels,
And when I see him sweep through towns and villages,
My heart starts throbbing,
Tears fill my eyes ....
With a brass plate at his front
And a red lamp hanging out,
He is always emerging out of smoke, carrying a thousand lives.

Flags and signals
Wave him on .... on shining rails in perfect order ....
To the back of this big and honest man
We raise our arms in eager praise.

SHIGEHARU NAKANO

From a Railway Carriage

Faster than fairies, faster than witches,
Bridges and houses, hedges and ditches;
And charging along like troops in a battle,
All through the meadows the horses and cattle:
All of the sights of the hill and the plain
Fly as thick as driving rain;
And ever again, in the wink of an eye,
Painted stations whistle by.

Here is a child who clambers and scrambles,
All by himself and gathering brambles;
Here is a tramp who stands and gazes;
And there is the green for stringing the daisies!
Here is a cart run away in the road
Lumping along with man and load;
And here is a mill and there is a river:
Each a glimpse and gone for ever!

ROBERT LOUIS STEVENSON

from **Journey**

Oh the wild engine! Every time I sit
In a train I must remember it.
The way it smashes through the air; its great
Petulant majesty and terrible rate:
Driving the ground before it, with those round
Feet pounding, beating, covering the ground;
The piston using up the white steam so
You cannot watch it when it come or go;
The cutting, the embankment; how it takes
The tunnels, and the clatter that it makes;
So careful of the train and of the track,
Guiding us out, or helping us go back;
Breasting its destination: at the close
Yawning, and slowly dropping to a doze.

HAROLD MONRO

The Night Mail

This is the night mail crossing the border,
Bringing the cheque and the postal order,
Letters for the rich, letters for the poor,
The shop at the corner and the girl next door,
Pulling up Beattock, a steady climb —
The gradient's against her but she's on time.

Past cotton grass and moorland boulder,
Shovelling white steam over her shoulder,
Snorting noisily as she passes
Silent miles of wind-bent grasses;
Birds turn their heads as she approaches,
Stare from the bushes at her blank-faced coaches;
Sheepdogs cannot turn her course,
They slumber on with paws across;
In the farm she passes no one wakes
But a jug in a bedroom gently shakes.

Dawn freshens, the climb is done.
Down towards Glasgow she descends
Towards the steam tugs, yelping down the glade of cranes
Towards the fields of apparatus, the furnaces
Set on the dark plain like gigantic chessmen.
All Scotland waits for her;
In the dark glens, beside the pale-green sea lochs,
Men long for news.

Letters of thanks, letters from banks,
Letters of joy from girl and boy,
Receipted bills and invitations
To inspect new stock or visit relations,
And applications for situations,
And timid lovers' declarations,
And gossip, gossip from all the nations,
News circumstantial, news financial,
Letters with holiday snaps to enlarge in,
Letters with faces scrawled on the margin.
Letters from uncles, cousins and aunts,
Letters to Scotland from the South of France,
Letters of condolence to Highlands and Lowlands,
Notes from overseas to the Hebrides;
Written on paper of every hue,
The pink, the violet, the white and the blue,
The chatty, the catty, the boring, adoring,
The cold and official and the heart's outpouring,
Clever, stupid, short and long,
The typed and the printed and the spelt all wrong.

Thousands are still asleep
Dreaming of terrifying monsters
Or a friendly tea beside the band at Cranston's or Crawford's;
Asleep in working Glasgow, asleep in well-set Edinburgh,
Asleep in granite Aberdeen.
They continue their dreams
But shall wake soon and long for letters.
And none will hear the postman's knock
Without a quickening of the heart,
For who can bear to feel himself forgotten?

W.H. AUDEN

The Freight Train

The slow freight wriggles along the rail
With a red caboose for a lashing tail,
With a one-eyed engine for a head
The slow freight follows the river bed.

He moves like a snake that has grown too fat
One that has swallowed a frog and a rat;
But a giant of snakes is the moving freight
And these are some of the things he ate:

A herd of sheep and a hundred hens
And dozens of pigs with crates for pens
And horses and cows by the sixes and tens;
And these are some of the things he drank:
Oil and gasoline by the tank,
Milk by the gallon and cream by the pail —
No wonder he moves at the pace of a snail.

ROWENA BASTIN BENNETT

Poetry Close-up

1. Christopher Hassall mentions Euston in his poem 'Puffing Billy'. What and where is Euston?

2. Read the poem 'The Night Mail' by W.H. Auden.
   a) To which country is the train travelling?
   b) What does the poet mean by 'The gradient's against her'?
   c) Which line in the poem tells us that the train causes vibration in people's homes?

3. Look at the poem 'The Freight Train' by Rowena Bastin Bennett.
   a) With what does the poet compare the movement of the train?
   b) Find out what a caboose is.

4. Imagine and write a conversation between an old steam-engine and the new diesel that is replacing it.

Other Things To Do

1. Describe how a simple steam-engine works.

2. What kinds of locomotives are used today?

3. Find out as much as you can about . . . . the Mallard . . . . the Deltic . . . . the High Speed Train . . . . The Advanced Passenger Train.

4. Find out about steam locomotives still in use in this country. Which is your nearest steam centre?

5. Choose one foreign railway and make a detailed study of it.

6. Read 'The Railway Children' by E. Nesbit.

By Water

'They have launched the little ship,
She is riding by the quay.'

In this section you will find some poets' thoughts on boats and ships.

Read the poems and think about these questions.

What types of craft use the sea?

.... Think of — luxury liners .... busy coastal freighters .... swift hovercraft .... huge tankers .... gaily-coloured yachts .... crowded ferries.

.... Think of — trips round the bay .... hauling in the nets .... dredging channels .... rescue at sea.

Do you enjoy travel by sea?

.... Think of — white-crested waves .... wind-blown spray .... salt-laden air .... churning wakes .... circling gulls .... rolling decks .... queasy stomachs.

If you wish to write your own poem, these words may help you.

bow	afloat	tide	depths	sunken	trough
buoyant	breaker	galleon	quay	biting	horizon
fresh	tranquil	soak	float	froth	bracing
port	storm	deck	cargo	starboard	dinghy

Sea Legend

There is a myth about the lost underwater city of Atlantis. Find out all you can about it.

Imagine you lived in this city. Describe your way of life and how the city disappeared.

If you turn to page 82 you will find some questions on the poems themselves and some more things to do.

Paper Boat

I made a little boat,
O, will she sink or float?
Upon the stream I sent her sailing, past
The gardens and the high banks very fast,
Her silver-paper sail and matchstick mast
Were quivering on that sullen winter tide
As she zigzagged and bumped from side to side,
A craft without a man on board to guide
Her safely on her voyage to the sea
Where other little boats are riding free;
She darted everywhere and rolled away from me,
And then, after a hundred yards or so,
Over a waterfall I saw her go
Stern over bow and quickly sink below.
I had a little boat,
I'm glad I saw her float.

LEONARD CLARK

A Baby Sardine

A baby sardine
Saw her first submarine:
She was scared and watched through a peephole.

'Oh, come, come, come,'
Said the sardine's mum,
'It's only a tin full of people.'

SPIKE MILLIGAN

A Flock of Little Boats

A flock of little boats
Tethered to the shore
Drifts in still water . . . .
Prows dip, nibbling.

SAMUEL MENASHE

Cargoes

Quinquereme of Nineveh from distant Ophir
Rowing home to haven in sunny Palestine,
With a cargo of ivory,
And apes and peacocks,
Sandalwood, cedarwood, and sweet white wine.

Stately Spanish galleon coming from the Isthmus,
Dipping through the Tropics by the palm-green
   shores,
With a cargo of diamonds,
Emeralds, amethysts,
Topazes, and cinnamon, and gold moidores.

Dirty British coaster with a salt-caked smoke stack
Butting through the Channel in the mad March days,
With a cargo of Tyne coal,
Road-rail, pig-lead,
Firewood, iron-ware, and cheap tin trays.

JOHN MASEFIELD

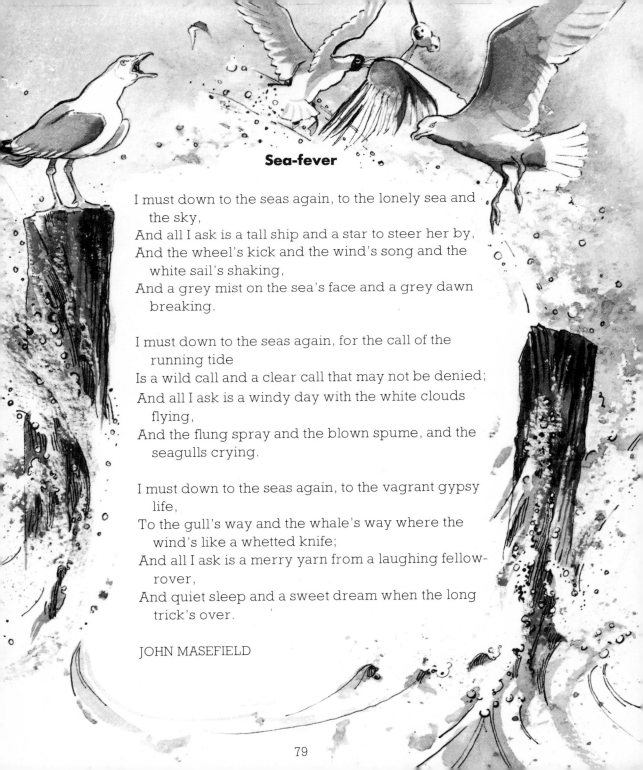

Sea-fever

I must down to the seas again, to the lonely sea and
    the sky,
And all I ask is a tall ship and a star to steer her by,
And the wheel's kick and the wind's song and the
    white sail's shaking,
And a grey mist on the sea's face and a grey dawn
    breaking.

I must down to the seas again, for the call of the
    running tide
Is a wild call and a clear call that may not be denied;
And all I ask is a windy day with the white clouds
    flying,
And the flung spray and the blown spume, and the
    seagulls crying.

I must down to the seas again, to the vagrant gypsy
    life,
To the gull's way and the whale's way where the
    wind's like a whetted knife;
And all I ask is a merry yarn from a laughing fellow-
    rover,
And quiet sleep and a sweet dream when the long
    trick's over.

JOHN MASEFIELD

The Ship

There was no song nor shout of joy
   Nor beam of moon or sun,
When she came back from the voyage
   Long ago begun;
But twilight on the waters
   Was quiet and grey,
And she glided steady, steady and pensive,
   Over the open bay.

Her sails were brown and ragged,
   And her crew hollow-eyed,
But their silent lips spoke content
   And their shoulders pride;
Though she had no captives on her deck,
   And in her hold
There were no heaps of corn or timber
   Or silks or gold.

J.C. SQUIRE

The Ship

They have launched the little ship,
   She is riding by the quay.
Like a young doe to the river,
   She has trembled to the sea.

Her sails are shaken loose;
   They flutter in the wind.
The cat's-paws ripple round her
   And the gulls scream behind.

The rope is cast, she moves
   Daintily out and south,
Where the snarling ocean waits her
   With tiger-foaming mouth.

RICHARD CHURCH

Legging the Tunnel

I don't know whether I believe
All Grandpa says;
Whether there ever really was
A tunnel
From side to side
Only an inch or so more wide
Than a canal boat;
Or that
Wrapped in a boatman's duffel coat
He had a ride
Under the Wren's Nest Hill.

The water, he said, lay black and still
When they cast off the horse,
And nosed the boat by pole
Into that dark, unwinking hole.

I can remember Grandpa's words:
'Out of a world of sky and trees and birds
We slid;
Out of the yellow sun
Into the rifled barrel of a gun
It seemed;
No path,
Only a tube
Of brickwork half awash with water
Where a shout
Bounced off the rounded, echoing roof
Ridged with worn bands
Of masonry;
Ribbed to the touch of groping hands
Like a knitted sleeve turned inside out.'

'Two miles of tunnel.'

'If you snuffed the lantern half-way through
And lost
The capering ogres on the walls
The blackness sucked and blew
In a whistle past you to a far pin-hole
    of light
The tunnel end.
You were alone
In a pipe of starless night;
Only the slap and chuckle of the water
    on the sides
As the boatman lay
Shouldering back on the cabin ramp
And walked the ceiling like a fly
With hob-nailed boots.
We were
Legging the tunnel.'

GREGORY HARRISON

Poetry Close-up

1. What name does Samuel Menashe give to the front of a boat?

2. In the poem 'The Ship' by J.C. Squire, can you find the name for where cargo is stored on board ship?

3. a) In Richard Church's poem, what are the 'cat's-paws'?

   b) What evidence do you find in this poem that the sea is rough?

4. From 'Cargoes', list the different ways in which the ships are powered.

5. Imagine you are on a sailing ship during a storm and hear the cry 'rocks ahead'. Describe the next hour.

Other Things To Do

1. Find out all you can about these sea mysteries and myths — Flannan Isle . . . . sea serpents . . . . mermaids.

2. Describe life on board a North Sea oil-rig.

3. What is the Plimsoll Line on a ship?

4. Find out about the work of the R.N.L.I.

5. Try to read one of these books — Treasure Island by R.L. Stevenson — Coral Island by R.M. Ballantyne — Twenty Thousand Leagues Under the Sea by Jules Verne.

By Air

'Aeroplane! Aeroplane!
Humming through the sky'

In this section you will find some poets' thoughts on aircraft and space travel. Read the poems and think about these questions.

What sort of aircraft fly in the sky?

.... Think of —noisy planes and graceful gliders ....
soaring kites and buzzing models ....
clattering helicopters and hot air
balloons.

Would you like to fly a plane?

.... Think of —winking lights .... thundering engines
.... take-off .... surrounding clouds
.... a bird's-eye view.

Can you imagine a journey in space?

.... Think of —spectacular launches and silent space
.... food tablets and weightlessness
.... space shuttles and orbiting
satellites .... re-entry and touchdown.

If you wish to write your own poem, these words may help you.

plunge	hangar	thrust	hurtle	meteoric	radar
hover	ascend	cockpit	crew	control	panoramic
altitude	whine	plummet	drove	taxi	supersonic
trundle	cargo	streamlined	whirring	propellor	aerial

Happy Landings

Find out what you can about the following people.

The Montgolfier brothers .... The Wright brothers .... Louis Bleriot .... Alcock and Brown .... Charles Lindbergh .... Frank Whittle .... Christopher Cockerell .... Yuri Gagarin .... Neil Armstrong.

If you turn to page 88 you will find some questions on the poems themselves and some more things to do.

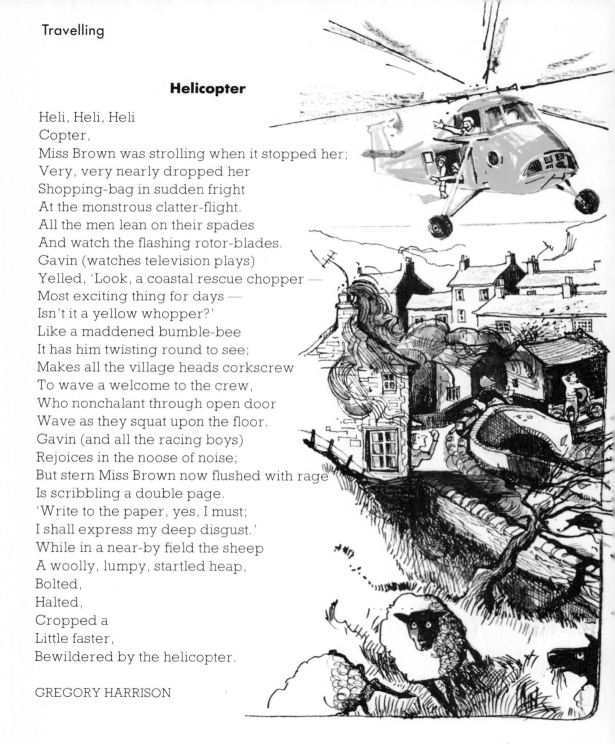

Helicopter

Heli, Heli, Heli
Copter,
Miss Brown was strolling when it stopped her;
Very, very nearly dropped her
Shopping-bag in sudden fright
At the monstrous clatter-flight.
All the men lean on their spades
And watch the flashing rotor-blades.
Gavin (watches television plays)
Yelled, 'Look, a coastal rescue chopper —
Most exciting thing for days —
Isn't it a yellow whopper?'
Like a maddened bumble-bee
It has him twisting round to see;
Makes all the village heads corkscrew
To wave a welcome to the crew,
Who nonchalant through open door
Wave as they squat upon the floor.
Gavin (and all the racing boys)
Rejoices in the noose of noise;
But stern Miss Brown now flushed with rage
Is scribbling a double page.
'Write to the paper, yes, I must;
I shall express my deep disgust.'
While in a near-by field the sheep
A woolly, lumpy, startled heap,
Bolted,
Halted,
Cropped a
Little faster,
Bewildered by the helicopter.

GREGORY HARRISON

The Helicopter

Along the rim of sea and sky
  The helicopter roars,
Ready to hover low and scoop
  The drowning from our shores.

A cavern in the side reveals
  Perched on his windy seat
The rescuer, who waves to us
  And dangles both his feet.

Suppose he fell, on the page of sea
  Splashing, an inky blotch;
He'd have to save himself, and that
  Would be some fun to watch.

IAN SERRAILLIER

The Aeroplane

Aeroplane! Aeroplane!
Humming through the sky
Like a giant insect —
How I wish that I could fly too.

Seagull! Seagull!
White kite of the cliff-top,
Dipping and swooping —
How I wish that I had your wings.

DEREK STUART

The Aeroplane

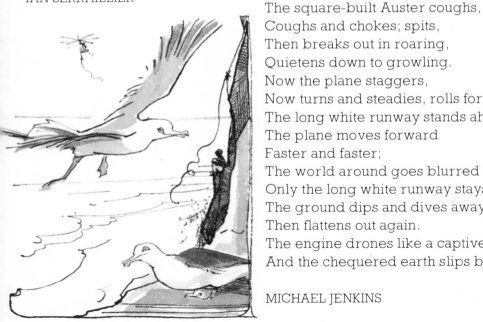

The square-built Auster coughs,
Coughs and chokes; spits,
Then breaks out in roaring,
Quietens down to growling.
Now the plane staggers,
Now turns and steadies, rolls forward.
The long white runway stands ahead.
The plane moves forward
Faster and faster;
The world around goes blurred with speed.
Only the long white runway stays,
The ground dips and dives away,
Then flattens out again.
The engine drones like a captive bee,
And the chequered earth slips by underneath.

MICHAEL JENKINS

Flying

I like to ride in my uncle's plane,
The one he pilots around the sky.
It's little and blue
And shiny, too,
And looks a lot like a dragonfly.

And once we're high in the summer air
With things below all shrunken in size,
It's easy to dream
How life would seem
If human beings were dragonflies.

The great wide river shrinks to a brook
That slowly winds away to the north,
Where ferries and tugs
Are water bugs
That skitter silently back and forth.

The faraway cows are just like ants,
And woods are patches of gray-green moss,
And telegraph lines
Where sunlight shines
Are glinting spider webs strung across.

It's quite exciting to hum through space
And view the world with an insect's eye.
A dragonfly-view
Makes things seem new,
Unless, of course, you're a dragonfly.

KAYE STARBIRD

Uncle

Uncle, whose inventive brains
Kept evolving aeroplanes,
Fell from an enormous height
On my garden lawn, last night.
Flying is a fatal sport,
Uncle wrecked the tennis-court.

HARRY GRAHAM

Space Travel

It won't be long before we catch
A rocket up to Mars
And spend the weekend visiting
Our friends upon the stars.
At Christmas when the days are cold
And the carol singers sing
We'll catch a rocket round the sun
And get a taste of Spring.

SYLVIA LEACH

Surprise! or the Escapologist

At the foot of the Apennine Mountains
Where the astronauts explore,
The curious Lunar Sea-squirt
Watches from its door.

And as they wander blithely
Around in their lunar cars,
The Sea-squirt steals their module
And flies away to Mars.

CAREY BLYTON

Poetry Close-up

1. In the poem 'The Aeroplane', of which insect might Derek Stuart be thinking?

2. Where do you think the helicopter is going in Gregory Harrison's poem?

3. In the poem by Michael Jenkins, which phrase does he use instead of saying the aeroplane lifts and soars away?

4. In the poem 'Flying' of what are the spider webs really made?

5. Which word in 'Uncle' tells us he was killed?

6. Where are the astronauts in the poem 'Surprise! or the Escapologist' by Carey Blyton?

7. Imagine you are flying in a plane. The pilot is taken ill, so you have to take over the controls. Tell the story.

Other Things To Do

1. Paint the insignia of some famous airlines, such as British Airways, Pan American, Quantas, Sabena, Lufthansa, Air Canada and Alitalia.

2. What jobs do these people do?
customs officer . . . . air hostess . . . . air controller . . . . flight engineer.

3. There are many unmanned satellites orbiting the Earth. What kind of tasks do they perform?